THE BEAUTY OF BETRAYAL

Overcoming God's Way

By Dr. Sandra B. Cook

*P*urpose*House*
Publishing

Dr. Sandra B. Cook has been in ministry for over twenty-eight years and is an author, investor, entrepreneur, mentor, and founder of the Church of Restoration and Transformation. She was an honor graduate of Benedict College, where she earned a Bachelor of Science in Accounting and continued her education to receive a Master's in Theology and a Doctorate in Ministry from Destiny Christian University, Winter Haven, Florida. She retired from the Social Security Administration in 2019 to become an author and a full-time apostle.

PurposeHouse Publishing
Columbia, Maryland
Visit our website at http://publishing.purposehouse.net.

For more information about the author, visit https://www.facebook.com/Dr-Sandra-B-Cook-101388414629586/.

Printed in the United States of America.

ISBN: 978-0-9963647-7-5

DEDICATION

I dedicate this book to my wonderful husband, Louis Cook, Jr., whose impressive submission to God has restored our family. I thank God for your support and allowing me to be who God has called me to be, even as a woman. I also dedicate this book to my sons, Justin and Louis III, for sharing me with so many other young people, and, even on Thanksgiving, allowing me to complete this book.

.

CONTENTS

ACKNOWLEDGEMENTS

I am grateful and thankful for my publisher, Lenita Reeves, of PurposeHouse Publishing. Thank you for your input and editing, designing, and marketing my book. My dreams became your priority, and I will forever be grateful.

To my mother: When God created you, he fearfully and wonderfully equipped you to deal with all of me. I am grateful for our intimate conversations. Thank you for helping me carry out the mandate for the church.

To my siblings: Arnold, Tommy, Yvonne, Bernard, Marilyn, Alexander, and Net, thank you all for the love, laughter, and support, and allowing me to be me outside the pulpit while respecting the mandate on my life in the pulpit.

To the Cook family: You all are the best! Thank you for sharing your brother with me.

To my spiritual leaders: Apostle Michael and Pastor Michelle Clinkscales, Pastor James and Co-Pastor Deborah White, and my dear friends Apostle Vernice Felder and Apostle Willette Salley, your words of advice fell on good ground. Thank you for your wisdom and revelation of truth.

To my God-children: Ashia Douglas, Carolina Redmond, and Corey J Brown, Jr., thank you for allowing me to be a part of your lives.

To my spiritual daughters: LaShonda Harper, Sarina Redmond, Makeitha Grigsby, and Tameka Green, my love for you inspired me to continue to write my life story. Shameka Flemming and Debra Myers, thank you for having a heart of gold and serving as family ambassadors to the younger generation.

To all my cousins, nieces, and nephews, I love you all. Now, keep it moving!

Last, to my church family, thank you all for growing with me and allowing me to lead you. We are better together!

Introduction

You can't always distance yourself from the people who betray you. Sometimes, you feel as if you are sleeping with the enemy, especially when someone in your trusted inner circle betrays you. And if you are a leader, God calls you to love the very people who will betray you.

We should recognize that betrayal is a part of life. But it never ceases to sting and take us by surprise. But it does not surprise God when someone betrays us, no matter how close they are to us. Jesus knew Judas would betray him.

People have betrayed me several times. Betrayal was the foundation of my upbringing. My father walked out on us when I was a small child, and I didn't meet him until I was eighteen. I wrote letters, but he never responded. His reason—he didn't want to pay child support, and he was bold enough to tell me. When that happens, something inside you dies—at least it feels like it. I was a leader, but I carried the shame and rejection of my father walking out on us. He was never a part of my life. Even now, I don't know anyone on his side of the family.

When people in my inner circle betrayed me, it forced me to deal with my father's rejection. I was so angry at those who betrayed me, but God was using the betrayal to force me to face myself. My father's betrayal and absence in my life set me up for unforgiveness, anger, the spirit of rejection, and the spirit of control.

Had I not experienced betrayal, I would never know that it can be a catalyst for deliverance—if you let God change your perspective. And that's what I hope this book does for you. I want you to take a healing journey with me as I recount the emotions, mistakes, and lessons learned in my own experiences with betrayal. If you walk with me, you will face some hard questions like:

- What weapons are you using to deal with your betrayal, and are they all godly?
- Is the betrayal bringing out things in you that need to change?
- Are you being accountable for what's in you, or just blaming your betrayer for everything?
- Are you able to exercise the kind of wisdom and restraint Jesus did in response to his betrayal?
- Are you willing to let go of unforgiveness?

- Are you willing to ride this process out—all the way—like Jesus rode the donkey and went all the way to the cross?

I also want to empower you to rise above betrayal the next time it comes knocking at your door because it will come again. God will give you supernatural strength to rise above it. He did it for me, and I know he can do it for you. Let's journey together through the pages of this book.

CHAPTER 1: PUT YOUR EMOTIONS IN CHECK

"Now what?" I heard a voice ask. "Now what?"

I laid there on the floor. My eyes were open, but I could not see the room. Something supernatural had surrounded me. It was like a thick fog that had consumed my vision.

"Now what are you going to do?" The voice asked again.

That night, my emotions boiled over. They were torrid, mixed, and raging; I could not control my sobbing. I helped other people manage their lives and put their emotions in check. But at that moment, I could not control mine. I didn't know where to begin or what to do to answer the question.

That Sunday, I pushed my way from the pulpit to the

5

front door of the church, and escaped the chatters and accolades about how great service had been. I made excuses along my way out, so others could not see the tears in my eyes. Service may have been great—but I wasn't.

After getting home that night, I locked the bedroom door and fell to the floor, exhausted from fighting within myself. I lay there sobbing, my emotions running wild. I couldn't take it anymore. We were having financial problems, my marriage was in crisis, and my teenage sons were struggling with their identity. My work environment was hostile, a so-called friend was trying to sabotage my ministry, and the people I expected to encourage me were siding with the so-called friend. On top of that, being an emotional eater did not help my situation; it only made it worse. I was gaining weight and did not recognize myself in the mirror. I was out of control!

On the surface, I was calm; but inwardly, my emotions were ablaze. That night, they exploded. After a turbulent display of crying and lamenting, the Holy Spirit said, "Now what? What are you going to do?"

That was the wake-up call I needed, the "Holy Ghost Check" that began my journey to healing. My emotions had been "out of whack" for some time. That's right. I preached that day, and nobody knew what was going on inside of me. I went on with my daily life, yet when I came home, I had to face myself, which wasn't easy.

It was easier for me to deal with other people's issues

because I could always give them a word from scripture to encourage them or help their situation. Even in my pain, I enjoyed helping others! When God calls you, you give so much of yourself because you genuinely want to help others. I had a word for everyone else's situation, but this time, I could not find a word for myself. Raging thoughts, emotions, and lack of faith overwhelmed me.

I had not dealt with my issues of rejection, unforgiveness, betrayal, manipulation, and control, but I was preaching powerful messages that delivered others and set them free. Yet, I was in bondage and ashamed. It was like trying to feast on a half-cooked meal. When you leave food undone (uncooked), you have nothing to eat, and so it is when there are unresolved issues in your life. Others were feasting from my sermons. Still, there were so many pots on the stove that needed my attention, and it left me paralyzed. I didn't know what to address first. I was overwhelmed, and I didn't know how to take my next breath much less how to handle one more issue in my life. So I ended up in the middle of the floor that night.

All of this turbulence was happening as we launched the ministry from the ground up. Not only did I face the usual pressures of starting a new ministry, but also everything else that was coming my way. I questioned God concerning my calling. I even searched for others to pastor the church, but God would not release me. With all the other issues, it did not help that I grew up Baptist and married a Catholic. I had previously worked at an African Methodist Episcopal (AME) church, but was ordained in the Church of God In Christ (COGIC) and had an apostolic calling on my life. I was trying to get a grasp on who God had called me to be while dealing with crises. There was frustration on top of frustration.

I am thankful for that night I laid in the middle of the floor. I realized I could not move forward without dealing with my emotions. My healing journey did not begin—and could not begin—until I put my emotions in check. I could never bring God glory in the state I was in that night. I could never move forward to my destiny, future, or purpose in life without first dying to my emotions. Like many of us, I would be living and even ministering but never experiencing the fullness of God operating in my life. I realized that a lot of the other symptoms I was dealing with stemmed from never being healed from betrayals. One of the hardest things for me to overcome was betrayal from my father, my husband, and someone I had let into my life as a trusted friend.

So I learned first-hand that to deal with betrayal, you must die to your emotions.

Sometimes, it is hard to detect a silent betrayer. They come under the guise of wanting to help, but they often misrepresent who they are around others. My mother nor my husband could explain what was causing the chaos and confusion between us, yet they knew something wasn't right. Have you ever been in conversation with someone, and no matter how hard you try to explain something, the conversation always seems to end with a blame game? My silent betrayer's agenda was to take the ministry, and no one around me could see it—not even my mother and my husband.

Initially, part of my pain was no one else saw the deceitful side of this person. There were times my family would tell me, "Don't be so hard on them," but they didn't know the full story. They were taking the person's side, and I felt like I was dying, both mentally and physically. The two people closest to me had denied me and sided with my betrayer who had intentionally targeted my family to turn them against me.

Betrayal starts in your inner circle, with those closest to you. Satan uses those near and dear to your heart, and that's why betrayal can be so painful. The enemy will use those that you trust the most to betray you. Why? Because you have already opened your heart to them, you trust them, and don't suspect them. Remember, you would never let people you don't trust close to what is precious to you. Thus, to touch what you value, the enemy has no choice but to use those closest to you.

Usually, after experiencing that kind of hurt, I would back away from people. My grandmother describes it as "feeding people with a long-handled spoon." When this happened before, I would have disappeared out of people's lives and justified it in Jesus' name. But to minister to the unlovely, I had to die to the propensity to withdraw and put up walls. When you are a leader, it requires you to minister to, heal, and deliver the very people who betray you. Every leader must know and understand that if they want to be effective in ministry. That's what I had to do.

How? I had to forget about myself. I had to rise above my negative thoughts, feelings, and self-will. I wanted to defend myself. However, part of my dying process (dying to my emotions) was not doing what I wanted to do anymore or what I felt like doing. I had to die to what I thought was best and sit in a place where God could get my attention. I needed to listen to what he had to say. To hear and obey what he was saying, I had to be quiet. It was a challenge to stay quiet, but I had to overcome my emotions once and for all.

You cannot hear God when your emotions are in charge.

If your emotions are in charge, raging like torrid waves, they create too much noise for you to hear God. I first had to put my emotions in check to listen to his still small voice. Even though betrayal is painful, take yourself out of the equation. Look at the situation from a different perspective to experience healing. Supernatural guidance is necessary so that God will get the glory.

> But Jesus answered them, saying, "The hour has come that the Son of Man should be glorified. [24] Most assuredly, I say to you, unless a grain of wheat falls into the ground and dies, it remains alone; but if it dies, it produces much grain. (John 12:23-24 NKJV)

Without supernatural guidance, we cannot die to ourselves and produce much grain.

Without a higher perspective, we will continue to

withdraw and run from the very people God designed to bring us to our destiny. Every time I ran, distanced myself, or withdrew because of betrayal, I lost relationships. I wasn't helping the people God had called me to help; I was running away from them because they had issues, and I thought those issues would negatively impact me. I wasn't whole enough to handle their hurt and my unhealed wounds at the same time.

Satan capitalizes on unhealed, festering emotional wounds.

When you experience betrayal, never forget that you have to maintain your sanctification. Keep your heart and your spirit pure because Satan capitalizes on unhealed, festering emotional wounds. If you are not careful, evil spirits will attach themselves to you during this period of pain and betrayal because you are open, vulnerable, and wounded.

Issues from my past contributed to my breaking down that night. That night I could see the real me—the broken me I really was. When I looked in the mirror, I saw a broken soul. But when I walked away, I became what everyone wanted me to be. Yet my spirit man was crying out for help. After doing this so long, little did I know I had taken on a spirit I was not ready to confront. Remember, I said spirits attach themselves to you if you don't deal with your issues. That night I wasn't just dealing with betrayal, the ministry, my job, my husband, my sons, or my mother. I was dealing with a spirit that had attached itself to my life! It was the spirit of Jezebel. I had made up my mind that I would not get hurt anymore by anyone, so I put up walls and took control over every area of my life. And I did it in Jesus' name.

Let me try to explain how the spirit of Jezebel attached itself to my life. My father left us when I was a small child, which contributed to my issues of rejection and control. To protect myself from feeling further rejection or abandonment, I developed a way of dealing with people to make sure I got the outcome I wanted. I would manipulate the situation to make sure I got my desired outcome. God had to show me all of that. He will show you things you need to see as well—if you are ready and honest with yourself.

Through the years, there were open gates in my soul that the devil capitalized on because I wanted to be in control of my life, mental state, and future. I manipulated to get what I wanted and felt I needed. In 2012, I had to come to grips with all these emotions and a spirit that did not want to loose me—a controlling, Jezebel spirit. That night was my epiphany, but all of that junk had already been inside of me. The time had come for me to deal with what was inside of me. I could no longer ignore it.

Deliverance can begin when you accept responsibility for negative emotions.

Sometimes, betrayal can be a catalyst for deliverance. It sure was for me! When someone betrays you, it's easy to focus on them and blame them for everything. But even during betrayal, God still holds us accountable for our stuff—our issues. He can use betrayal to bring things out

of us, and to bring healing to our lives if we let him—
that's part of the beauty of betrayal I want to reveal to
you.

God can use betrayal to bring things
out of us and to bring healing to our
lives if we let him—that's part of the
beauty of betrayal I want to reveal to
you.

I began to ask the Holy Spirit to reveal areas in my life
that needed healing. The Holy Spirit revealed control,
rejection, bitterness, unforgiveness, and pride. I began to
read the scripture and ask God to deliver me from them
all; especially, control over my husband and my life!

The word of God sanctifies. It is the washing of the water
of the word of God that cleanses us. In times of betrayal,
hold on to the word of God. My sanctification continued
as I began to "read the red." For about four months, I
read what was in red ink only; meaning, the words of
Jesus highlighted in red, in *Red Letter Bibles*. I began to
look at Jesus more closely. By "reading the red," I saw
how he handled his disciples, the sick, the demon-
possessed, and afflicted.

Jesus didn't run from people. He embraced them! He
used wisdom to deal with them accordingly, and that
helped me to better deal with the people in my life. It
became easier for me to deal with those that had

betrayed me. The words of Jesus were cleansing my emotions, and wisdom was entering my heart.

Because of the words of Jesus (in red), I now had an answer to the question the Holy Spirit asked me that night. I had a response to the "Now what?" question because I now had Jesus' example. I saw the wisdom in operation in his life and how he handled people. The Spirit led him, and we also have to allow the Holy Spirit to lead us when we deal with people. Not only did I have to deal with people but also with myself.

Let the Holy Spirit lead you about how and what to minister to people. That includes what to say, how to say it, what to pray, and what to do. You may be the one planting a seed. You may not be the one to get them delivered, but you may be the one to speak a word of encouragement.

Whatever the case, during your betrayal and healing, you will find wisdom in the scriptures. The word of God will renew your mind and anchor your emotions. It will also help you see your accusers from a different perspective, which is what we discuss in the next chapter.

✓ **Keep your emotions in check! Don't hate your accusers.**

Chapter 2: Don't Hate Your Accusers

"Be careful. Use wisdom," my sister said just before she walked out of the room.

A few days later, she said, "Get your oil. Let's pray. Something is about to happen, and you need wisdom. You've got a long road ahead."

I didn't fully understand it, but God was using my sister to send what I call "little nuggets of warning." God was speaking through her, and she was preparing me for what was to come. I didn't know it was my betrayal and burial—my dying to myself and my emotions. Jesus went through a similar anointing before his burial (his death on the cross).

> While Jesus was in Bethany in the home of Simon the Leper, [7] a woman came to him with an alabaster jar of very expensive perfume,

which she poured on his head as he was reclining at the table. [8] When the disciples saw this, they were indignant. "Why this waste?" they asked. [9] "This perfume could have been sold at a high price and the money given to the poor." [10] Aware of this, Jesus said to them, "Why are you bothering this woman? She has done a beautiful thing to me. [11] The poor you will always have with you, but you will not always have me." [12] *When she poured this perfume [fragrant oil] on my body, she did it to prepare me for burial.* (Matthew 26:6-12 NIV, emphasis added)

God sent his son into this world, knowing that we would betray him, and he would suffer a horrible, painful death. He knew who would betray Jesus, and who would come into his journey to the cross to anoint him and prepare him for death. Likewise, God also knew that you and I would experience betrayal. He knew who would betray us, and who would come into our lives to anoint and strengthen us to go through the experience.

God knows you will experience betrayal and who will betray you. He's not surprised.

Remember, God knew you before you knew yourself. He knows you by name, and he's not taken by surprise by the happenings in your life. I had to shift my mindset and realize that God already knew who would betray me. When my biological sister told me, "Be careful. Use wisdom," he was sending a warning. The betrayal wasn't a surprise to him.

I had to accept that God allowed it, and as a result, I had to go through it and let it happen. Once I acknowledged that my perspective changed, and I realized that although it was painful, the betrayal would make me better. Then, I understood that I had to go through it not only to be a better person but also to see the nature of God and my betrayer's character differently.

Embrace a different perspective. See your accusers differently.

Everyone wants to know God as Jehovah Jireh, the provider—we all want our needs met. But there are different characteristics of God. He is a refiner, purifier, and sanctifier.

But who may abide the day of his coming? and who shall stand when he appeareth? *for he is like a refiner's fire, and like fullers' soap:* (Malachi 3:2 KJV, emphasis added)

God used the betrayal so I could know him as "God my Sanctifier," "God my Purifier," and "God my Peace." As I focused on God, I could finally see that the betrayal wasn't so much about the evil in the other person, but what God wanted to clean up in me. I had to take my focus off my accusers and embrace the attributes of God. He was the protector of my mental state, keeping me in perfect peace during emotional storms.

It was a two-year journey: It wasn't overnight. Eventually, I considered my accusers as necessary elements of the process that was drawing me closer to God. To go through the betrayal, I had to go to a deeper level in God. I had to understand that it was a process that unfolded so I could become better and remove the bitterness from my childhood. I needed to see others through God's eyes.

If you are experiencing betrayal, know that it's bigger than you. God's the master, and he's sovereign. He knows how to use the situation to bring glory to himself and mature you. It is humbling, but remember, God will send warning signs. Even though betrayal is humbling, God will not leave you humiliated.

Choose humility.

I say this from experience because the people who betrayed me were not only a part of my inner circle but also a part of my destiny. Learn how to overcome what people think, even when it will cause you to appear weak. Learn how to humble yourself, even if you must take a demotion. At one time in my career, I took a demotion to put distance between my accusers and me. Taking the low road doesn't mean you are wrong. It means you are not willing to forfeit God's plan for your life. People may see it one way, but God sees it as part of the process to bring you to a place of destiny. I would have never written this book if I had not taken the low road.

When I left one of my jobs, some people were trying to figure out why I didn't put up a fight. Others thought I was guilty because I didn't fight. Whatever they thought, I thank God for every one of them. My pain, pressure, and persistence helped me "continue down the path of righteousness for his name's sake." (Psalm 23:3) I could not hate or blame my accusers. Instead, I humbled myself, fasted, and prayed. The times of fasting helped me get past what was happening. Years later, everyone learned the truth, and because I humbled myself, my character was still intact.

There is more to the beauty of betrayal. In another situation, an accuser entered the ministry. They would go to my mother and speak negative things to bring a stigma to my name. When a deceiver wants to betray you, he or she will use any means necessary to bring you down; and on a bigger scale, to bring the kingdom of God down. That is why you cannot afford to give way to the enemy.

My husband had followed the crowd and became an accuser. Our ministry was in jeopardy, I could have stopped it, called them all together, and exposed my betrayer, but that is not how God allowed me to do it. He wanted me to focus on him instead of responding to the accuser. It helped build my character.

God allowed it so I could draw closer to him. During that time, I had to learn how to worship him, humble myself, and bow down. In my humility, he released strength. He anointed me to go through the process.

He will anoint you to go through your process.

When my biological sister first met one of my betrayers, God revealed their motives to her quickly—even before he showed me! God also used her to anoint me for the process. She would tell me, "Be careful. Use wisdom."

During that season, I felt there was something different about my house. The Lord told me to anoint my house. One day, I stayed home from work and anointed my home from the ceilings and cabinets to the floors. Then he said, "Now, anoint yourself." That experience helped me see the importance of anointing myself and things around me.

There is strengthening in anointing yourself that you can't see, a supernatural power that comes to allow you to deal with life at another level. Through the anointing, you don't even know how you get through things; but it is the strengthening, wisdom, peace, and joy of God.

By his strengthening, I overcame bitterness and resentment. The process took two years because I thought I had the right to be resentful. But as I continued to focus on God in worship and his word, I became better—and not bitter.

Specifically, I became better at being slow to speak. I intentionally didn't say a lot. I may have seemed weak because I wasn't speaking out to defend myself, but I was using wisdom not to say things I would later regret.

I definitely had to bring revelation to my mother because she believes in hospitality. She would feed people and have the whole church over to her house every week if she could. But not everybody that comes to your hangout has good intentions. Judas betrayed Jesus within the boundaries of what he called home. She tried to explain to me, "You shouldn't treat [this person] like this; they're a nice person." My mom continued to scold me. She went in on me, bringing up things from my early childhood. As she was talking, I thought, "Why is she going back to my childhood? Could there be something that she knows that I don't know?"

Again, my mother continued. I replied, "One day, you will learn the truth." I didn't tell her everything about my betrayer. She didn't know the person was talking to my husband and contacting my children. I said nothing. It was not my battle; I just said, "One day, you will learn the truth." I didn't allow the accusations to go to the root of my soul.

I would not take it out on my mother because she didn't understand everything that was going on. I didn't defend my character. I would not get into a debate or go back and forth, but the devil was using my accuser in ways my family didn't understand or recognize.

Like a wolf in sheep's clothing, a betrayer knows how to blend in with others—they know exactly what to say and how to say it to keep from giving themselves away before their time. Like most betrayers, they have a plan—an ulterior motive. They play the victim and never the victor. They try to control you, and when they see that they cannot, they use the closest people around you.

Betrayers and deceivers normally maneuver for three things:

1) Influence through Position

They want higher positions in the workplace, church, or amongst people. In my experience, to gain the position, they discredited my leadership abilities and often made notes of things that went wrong. Even though God had appointed me to lead, they felt they could do a much better job. Usually, their pride led to disrespect.

2) Influence through Power

Like Judas, they strategically planned ways to get more power and influence through money. Sometimes, when people have wealth, they use it as a tool to gain goodwill and blessings from others. They feel that carrying the money bag is a sign of success, righteousness, and a deeper and stronger relationship with God. But that's far from the truth. Merit is not the basis of a relationship with God. Be ready to go on a warpath when you don't accept their advice, gifts, or money. They lose control over your life when you don't give them leverage by taking their money.

3) Influence over the Promise

They will never bring you into their inner circle, but they will want to connect to yours. They will rebel against the vision of the church or denounce every promise God has planned for you to bring about their vision. They may give threats of leaving, but they will not go until you ignore their threats. Just like Judas, Jesus' betrayer, your circle of friends may never know they are the secret betrayer. I think you call that deception! Make sure you know the truth about those around you.

During one betrayal, my relationship with my inner circle became very strenuous. The accuser was playing on my family's emotions, and I couldn't stand to see it! My family thought they were helping, but they were only making a pathway for the adversary.

This person was building their story—one victim story after another, after another. Eventually, my husband felt sorry for them and defended their behaviors. Their influence on my husband made the truth a lie and a lie the truth.

It was extremely painful, and I could not retaliate because it could have damaged my whole family. It would have been easier if it wasn't my inner circle. When it's the outer circle, you can walk away or not entertain it; but because it was my inner circle, it forced me to deal with it. I could not avoid it.

Don't hate your accusers.

Betrayal doesn't take God by surprise. We get comfortable with God working things out a certain way, but God doesn't always operate the way we expect. He used betrayal to get Jesus to the cross to fulfill his destiny, and he can do the same with us. Remember, God can use anyone to change us for the better, including deceivers, betrayers, and accusers.

Embrace betrayal from a different perspective. Don't hate your accusers–love them because God sent them to take you on a "path of righteousness for his name's sake." We often want to move into a deeper, more intimate relationship with God, but how do we do that? By allowing God to get all the mess out of us, we gain access to go to the next level. Take a moment to ask God to show you the areas of brokenness that the root of betrayal has caused in your life and for the grace to confront them.

Take a moment to ask God to show you the areas of brokenness that the root of betrayal has caused in your life and for the grace to confront them.

 All my betrayers helped me to see what was inside of me. At forty-eight, betrayal forced me to deal with my issues for the first time. I had to forgive my father repeatedly. I had to forgive my husband repeatedly, and I had to forgive my in-laws, family, and friends. If I would be an effective leader, I had to forgive even those that tried to destroy the ministry by speaking negative words.

If you shift your focus, you will see God from a different perspective.

Choose humility. God will anoint you and strengthen you to go through the betrayal process. I learned not to hate the people God was using to make me wiser and smarter. The scripture declares, "… all things work together for good to them that love God, to them who are the called according to his purpose." (Romans 8:28 KJV) So if we love him and believe God called us, we have to allow him to work the bad (betrayal) for our good.

"All things" includes betrayal. If we believe the word of God, we have to believe all of it—in good and in bad. Believe God's word, stand on it, and speak it.

Let the word of God cleanse you, but don't let betrayal change you for the worst.

✓ **KEEP YOUR EMOTIONS IN CHECK! DON'T LET BETRAYAL CHANGE YOU.**

CHAPTER 3: DON'T LET IT CHANGE YOU

"Someone's here to see you," my mom said.

I walked in and saw a man sitting there.

"You're my dad? Did you get any of my letters? What brings you here now?" I asked.

My dad had walked out on us when I was less than a year old. I had never seen him before, and now at eighteen, he wanted to walk into my life, how dare him! I had already graduated from high school, and he didn't even come to my graduation—the nerve of him. I wrote letters but didn't get one letter in return, so I stopped writing letters to him when I was sixteen.

Even though he abandoned us, my mom never allowed us to talk badly about him, and she would make us call him on his birthday. That day, she welcomed him into the house. I thought, "This man walked out on you with your best friend. Why are you welcoming him?"

"You're eighteen now. I don't have to pay child support," he said.

"You never paid child support," I replied.

That's one of the reasons I moved around so much. I thought your mom would make me pay child support," he replied.

"You know what, that's fine. Nice to meet you." I walked out of the room.

I never tried to resolve the issue with my father. I just carried the issue. That's why the spirit of rejection operated in my life.

Amid the betrayals that transpired at work and church, I had unresolved insecurities from my dad not being a part of my life as a child—my first, severe betrayal. I was at a breaking point, and I remember saying, "God, this is really more than I can handle." Because of my dad, I secretly dealt with rejection all my life. That latest betrayal had brought the issue to the surface and magnified it.

I didn't have to see my father all those years, so the rejection stayed under the surface. I realized that, because of what he did, I looked for love and acceptance in other people. Other people didn't know that because I always played hard. I would always be the one to respond with words that could tear a person apart.

The rejection was changing me.

I was guarding myself against hurt or the possibility of getting hurt. If I could say certain things to you, then I could tell that you loved me because my words could cut. It was one way I put up walls because of hurt and rejection, versus letting people in my life.

That's why when I dated, I had issues with men. I liked men, but I always had an unspoken expectation that whoever I dated was going to leave me too. Inwardly, I would think, "He's going to cheat too." It was the bitterness from my dad leaving me.

I didn't know how to respect men. I had to control them; they would not control me or hurt me the way my dad hurt me. I always felt I had to do things myself, and I had severe trust issues. I lived my life like I didn't need any man I was dating. Certainly, they would not tell me what to do. These attitudes resulted from unresolved pain from my father leaving.

I was still dealing with the rejection and abandonment and putting up walls. So when the person in the church betrayed me, it was painful because I rarely let anybody get that close to me (besides my family). I don't know how this person got into my life like that.

Insecurities from my past, coupled with betrayal from others, could have caused me to doubt myself as a leader. The things they were saying about me hurt. I could have shrunk under the ridicule and questioned my call to lead the church.

But I couldn't denounce who I was. I couldn't let the betrayal and rejection change me. Yet, it had until the day I had lain on the floor in a foggy room. I had to allow God to deal with me.

Don't let it change you.

I refused to believe I was incapable of doing what God called me to do—to be a pastor and a wife. I still had to cook, clean, pay bills, etc., even when my husband was siding with my betrayer.

There was a strain on our marriage because my husband was siding with my betrayer. This person knew me and my husband were having problems, so they focused on that negative seed, watered it, and helped it to grow. Meanwhile, everything was coming to a boiling point in our marriage. They were getting the results they wanted and becoming overly aggressive towards me. I slowly backed away from the relationship and stopped all contact with the betrayer.

Notice I used the words, slowly? If you are not careful, a person like that can change you, damage your character, and ruin your reputation. I must admit, they knew their game and played it well. But you can't beat the Holy Spirit. He will bring all things to your remembrance and give you strategies to conquer the grave.

I had to stand, and do all to stand. I had to put myself in remembrance of who I was when God first called me into the ministry. I could not afford to change into what anybody else wanted or expected me to become; or what my pain was telling me to become (bitter, angry, and resentful). I refused to change into an angry, bitter monster.

I refused to change into an angry, bitter monster.

So I tell you, do not denounce who you are.

Don't let your insecurities nor the pain of betrayal turn you into a different person. Stay true to yourself, even while being misrepresented and accused. You are still the same person God called, appointed, and anointed for ministry.

Stay true to what the word of God says about you. Hold fast to who he called you to be amid accusation, misrepresentation, and all the other things going on around you. He who called you is faithful.

Don't let the betrayal process weaken your resolve. Stand on the word of God, and don't compromise his word because of accusations. Continue to correct and rebuke. Don't let the enemy capitalize on your situation to bring chaos and confusion. You must still lead and govern by the word of God and speak the truth—even when it hurts.

When God first gave us the church, I had a network of ministers around me. Everybody had an idea for me. I lost a lot of Christian leaders when I didn't adapt to their way of ministering, and accusers even came from that. But I still had to speak the word of God and speak the truth.

There were things people wanted to do in the church, but they were contrary to the scriptures. Even though my family members were telling me not to be so hard, I had to stand on the word and bring correction.

Always keep the word of God before you.

In that season, I needed the word of God to keep my sanity and not lose focus. I did not leave the house without consuming the word of God. I allowed it to be my breakfast. He established my day in that prayer time, and my eyes were open to the word of God throughout the day. I had to develop a deeper relationship with God and his word.

Unresolved rejection and bitterness can turn you into another person. But God's word is an anchor to your soul—your emotions. It cleanses and heals, and it simultaneously reinforces who you are in God's eyes.

His word will keep you from letting the betrayal change you. If you stand on the word of God, you will come out of the betrayal stronger and better. And the betrayal will not change who you are or cause you to demote yourself to a lesser version of who God called you to be.

Don't denounce who you are. Always keep the word of God before you.

The word of God is a primary weapon in the fight to overcome betrayal. However, there are other carnal weapons that you have to relinquish to overcome betrayal. We'll discuss them in the next chapter.

> ✓ **Keep your emotions in check! Lay down your weapons.**

Chapter 4: Lay Down Your Weapons

Have you accepted that your fight is not with people? Do your actions (and reactions) reflect that you have or have not? God's word is a weapon, but are you in the right fight?

You are not fighting the person who is betraying you. You wrestle not against flesh and blood.

For though we walk in the flesh, we do not war after the flesh: [4] (For the weapons of our warfare are not carnal, but mighty through God to the pulling down of strong holds;) [5] Casting down imaginations, and every high thing that exalteth itself against the knowledge of God, and bringing into captivity every thought to the obedience of Christ; [6] And having in a readiness to revenge all disobedience, when your obedience is fulfilled. (2 Corinthians 10:3-6 KJV)

Because of rejection and bitterness, I had developed

personal, self-protecting carnal weapons. I would cut you with my words before you could cut me. No one could get close to me unless they accepted a few lashes to prove their love.

God began to convict me. He told me, "Lay down your weapons." Emotionally, I was in distress. God was stripping away my trusted armor. As a result, I turned to food and began to eat those stressful emotions. I didn't have my weapons, so I turned to food. In less than a year, I had gained over forty pounds.

That was the first time I had to lay down every ounce of reassurance I had concerning how to fight and overcome. I had to lay down my carnal weapons: my words, thoughts, and manipulative actions. Those were my weapons. I knew how to manipulate people, but I had to lay down all my weapons. I had to die to my weapons.

My words were a weapon.

You must learn to use caution with the words you speak over people, especially when you're a leader. Betrayal causes you to see a person in one light, but God may still see him or her as his child, who will later repent. You may not know what God will do in and through a person's life. I would say things about my betrayers that I should not have, not realizing I was putting my words on a person's life. Betrayal forced me to confront this lethal weapon.

My thoughts were a weapon.

I would judge people and not even know it. I had a religious picture of righteousness. If I felt that what I saw in other people was not the righteousness of God, I would judge them—not knowing that I was still looking at things from the perspective of my past hurts. I failed in areas where I could have helped people; I walked away from them, or I judged them too soon.

My manipulative actions were a weapon.

Before beating the floor that night, I carried the spirit of Jezebel: I had to be in control of everything. Being in control was my defensive strategy to get things done my way. I would behave that way, primarily with my husband. If I wanted something done, and he didn't do it, I would be silent until he did. I would always "paint a picture" as if I was the victim. And because I knew both his strengths and weaknesses, I would make things seem a certain way to get him to do it a certain way. I'm being very transparent, which may be too much information for some. But for others that need a breakthrough, I want to keep it real and be helpful.

I have overcome by the blood of the lamb and the word of my testimony! It is time to come clean and drop your weapons if you want God to heal you, your marriage, and your children. Jezebel is not a gender but a spirit that wants to control. Now, I can spot that spirit quicker than any other, why? Because God delivered me from it, so I walk with eagle eyes to see it and dismantle it.

If God has placed you in authority over a ministry, that is not a controlling spirit. That is a mandate to carry out that ministry God's way—not the way of man. A person with a controlling spirit tries to put themselves in another person's seat. As for my husband, he has the responsibility to govern our home. I was out of order all that time, but thinking my husband was out of order.

For example, I could have money already set aside; but if I wanted him to pay for something, I would paint a particular picture. That's something that I did not realize until I drew closer to God. I would always focus on what my husband did incorrectly, but not what I was doing wrong. I was never the bad one. I had ways to shield and defend myself. I was walking in self-righteousness until God began to let me see and accept my wrongdoings.

I didn't realize how much I had bruised my son. My mother taught me to be strong, but, as I later learned, it was not all good. My mother taught the girls to use defenses typical of men—not women. She taught us how to be strong because she had to be strong in raising her children without our father. I took control of areas that I should never have as a wife. My son grew up seeing me take the lead in many areas and thought that was the disposition of all women.

So he would put the same guard up; he didn't look at females as ladies because I had put up the façade of a man. I had a very strong personality. I had to drop my weapons in that area.

I had a dream, and in that dream, God told me to lay down my weapons. I was taking all these things off. I was reaching for things and laying them down. He said,

"Now, there's one more." "I've laid everything down," I replied. He pointed to my socks, and there was something in my socks.

From that dream, I began to see the people around me that I was hurting. Sometimes we carry secret weapons, without knowing. God had to point out that there were still other things I needed to lay down.

You will die, but you won't die.

As I let go, I felt weak and vulnerable. It felt as though I would die. I thought, "They're going to see that I have no strategies or methods." I wasn't retaliating. Instead, I was saying things like, "Let's take it to God." I now depended on God more than ever because I didn't have my old weapons anymore. That is a scary place to be. I was dying to my old ways.

Without the weapon of control, I wasn't sure I would win. I started to give up on the ministry and my marriage because it was such an uncomfortable, unfamiliar place to be. When I had to give the battle to God, I felt like I would not win. It forced me to walk by the Spirit and trust God without being able to control the situation.

I had to die to myself. It felt like I would physically die, but God had my back. He would give me the strength to declare, "I can't give up. I got to keep moving." Don't try to figure out why or how you will win without your old weapons. Embrace God's weapons and keep it moving! In the process, you will die to your past, selfish ways, but you won't die because he's preparing you for a higher level.

The "Greater One" is inside you.

I couldn't give up. I had to keep moving. The "Greater One" was inside of me, but he was also working something greater in my character as I walked with him. To get through the stripping process, I had to rely on the presence of God inside me. I had to focus on what he was working on in my character. I had to go through the process without relying on my flesh.

Likewise, there's greatness on the inside of you, and God wants to work it out of you. Your greatness must emerge to manifest his glory. You must talk, walk, and move like Christ. That requires laying down your weapons. Then, you will see and hear what he did in situations and respond to people as he responded.

Endure the stripping away and allow the Holy Spirit to work on the inside of you. If you don't master this lesson well, you will not be thoroughly equipped for the next challenge. Remember, the devil tempted Jesus in the wilderness, and the devil left him only for a season.

After the betrayer left my church, challenges didn't stop. Another set of people attacked, which is another reason we must allow betrayal to make us better. We need to be equipped because of new challenges and new people who will come.

Betrayal magnified my carnal weapons and forced me to

confront them. My weapons were negative words, thoughts, and manipulative actions.

God wants to deal with your negative weapons, whatever they may be. He holds us accountable even when we face betrayal. He wants to work out the greatness in you, and that requires letting go of things that will block your greatness.

As a result of laying down my weapons, I saw myself in the mirror, but a new person was looking back at me. Without all the rejection and bitterness, I was becoming a better, wiser version of myself. I could hold my tongue and stand still and see the salvation of the Lord. I could recognize the warning signs of betrayal and use wisdom.

I was learning to appreciate the new person looking back at me in the mirror, as well as the process I had to endure.

As a result of laying down my weapons, I saw myself in the mirror, but a new person was looking back at me.

If you learn how to lay down our weapons, stress and bitterness will not overtake you. The Holy Spirit will lead you, and you'll be able to deal with any Judas that tries to come into your inner circle. You'll be able to speak the truth in love and wisdom (without carnal weapons) to expose the enemy.

> ✓ **KEEP YOUR EMOTIONS IN CHECK! EXPOSE THE ENEMY.**

Chapter 5: Expose the Enemy: Recognize the Warning Signs

Laying down your weapons doesn't mean you allow the betrayer to continue to operate. It means you have nothing negative going on inside you. When you expose the betrayer, you're not retaliating but speaking the truth in love to bring correction, and protect your investment, loved ones, and in my case, the congregation. There are times you must expose the betrayer to protect your family or organization.

It's difficult to think of someone as a deceiver when you have liked them, genuinely loved them, chosen them, and brought them into your inner circle. They may operate without your detection because, in your mind, the thought of them betraying you is absurd. Your care for them makes it painful even to consider that they would deceive you.

A lot of times, I was in denial, not wanting to believe that someone I had loved was trying to block the progress of the ministry. But I learned that you need the wisdom to know and understand that someone is being used to oppress and attack you.

I had to use wisdom to confront the people who were attacking God's church and his will. Also, I had a concern for the congregation members.

There were people I allowed to sing, preach in the pulpit, or operate in ministry only to realize they were doing it for their agenda. So I had to protect the sheep. I needed God's wisdom to keep the innocent ones from being damaged and let them know there were wolves in sheep's clothing around.

By his grace, God revealed warning signs for potential betrayers and deceivers. He would send specific warnings or allow me to know that what they were doing was against how and what he said. He also let me know that if I allowed what they were doing to continue, I would be accountable. Thankfully, God would allow me to see certain things about a person. And even if I liked them, he would not allow me to promote them.

I would overhear discussions that revealed that there was something wrong. God kept me from stumbling, even with my inner circle. I was letting my guard down with them, not realizing that even in my inner circle, I had to be careful.

As a leader, I had to recognize the warning signs.

Maybe you've heard this before? "Pastor, God sent me

here to help you. How can I help?" There are warning signs that everyone should learn, but if you are a senior church leader, this section will be helpful to you in particular.

You find one of the biggest areas of betrayal and deception amongst the "called ones." I have assisted many pastors and apostles, and I never worked against their agendas. If the leader said to go left, I went left. If they said to go right, I went right. Why? Because like Elijah and Elisha, the leader carries the anointing to take you to the next level. I always believed in the anointing on the relationship between Elijah and Elisha.

My leaders taught me to work under someone else's anointing and to serve until they release you with a blessing. I did not want any of God's blessings cut off from me. You can't work two ministries out of one ministry. That also applies to husbands and wives. Work as one unto the Lord.

If God sends you to a place, work until the leader releases you. If you get an assignment, thank God for it; but never try to work your ulterior assignment in on God's time. He will not raise you up and send you out until experience equips you to work with lions, tigers, and bears. The pulpit is not the place to deceive the people with your agenda.

Now more than ever, the leaders in God's kingdom have to protect the people of God from wolves. Wolves want the platforms to show others what they can do—what a dangerous place to be without the grace, anointing, and

Spirit of God.

Leaders, if you give an assignment to your people and they cannot follow simple instructions, please be careful. You could be dealing with deception! For where a man's heart is, so is he. If their heart is not with the ministry, the best thing to do is to let them find another church home. Deception will eventually lead to betrayal. If not dealt with properly, it could cause problems in the ministry "down the road."

Leaders, you must be watchful and learn to take on the "bye-bye spirit." Even if you would like to see your ministry grow, building it with deception is not a strong foundation. I had to learn how to say, "I release you to do whatever God has called you to do."

Many members may be there with you, but they are not all following you. I truly understand the importance of walking as Elijah and Elisha walked. Elisha was preparing for Elijah's departure. Nowadays, deceivers want the platform and not the preparation.

Expose the enemy. Recognize the warning signs of betrayal.

There are warning signs that I call "Ds." Watch out for these five "Ds": disrespect, dishonesty, disobedience, double vision, and deception. I recommend that you study them so you can protect your labor, investments, and loved ones.

Disrespect

My betrayer's pride often led to disrespect through statements like, "I was sent here to help you, but you don't want my help." They became very aggressive and disrespectful in their approach and communication with me. In the same that way Lucifer thought he could be God; their disrespect was a sign that they thought I was not capable and could do a better job. Just like Lucifer, the disrespect was an outward display of what they had said in their hearts.

> How art thou fallen from heaven, O Lucifer, son of the morning! how art thou cut down to the ground, which didst weaken the nations! [13] **For thou hast said in thine heart,** I will ascend into heaven, I will exalt my throne above the stars of God: I will sit also upon the mount of the congregation, in the sides of the north: [14] I will ascend above the heights of the clouds; **I will be like the most High.** [15] Yet thou shalt be brought down to hell, to the sides of the pit. (Isaiah 14:12-15 KJV, emphasis added)

Dishonesty

Questions expose dishonesty. I would give assignments, and I knew they were uncompleted. But instead of accepting it, I would question why it didn't get done (even though I knew they had their plan). I confronted by asking questions.

They would lie, try to cover up, or make excuses for not getting it done. But many people would hear their response and know that it wasn't the spirit of God. I didn't have to make a scene. I just "called them to the carpet." Their dishonest answers exposed their hearts.

For some individuals, once I gave them a more glamourous assignment, I saw a change in them. After they got the microphone or got their certificate to preach, they focused on their agenda.

Disobedience

If they can't obey you, they stand a chance of betraying you. Women may use emotional trips to justify their disobedience more than men. Men may try to gather other men and make you doubt your calling because you are a woman. Whatever the case, if they disobey you, they can betray you. Be sure your inner circle and close assistants are people who will follow your instructions and not justify doing things their way.

Double Vision

Some people will come to help you with their own vision. They want to be there with you, but they can't let go of their vision (even if it's not the time). Free them and let them go. They cannot work two visions; that's called double vision. And a person can never see clearly with double vision. They will always go back and forth, causing the ministry to suffer. The people will not know which vision they are to carry out.

You may want them there to help build the ministry, but the longer you wait, the more the vision will suffer. It will eventually divide the people, and you might lose some casualties. Remember, each body has only one head. They will only be able to carry out one vision, yours or theirs.

I thank God for the warning signs. Because betrayers can say one thing with their mouth, but their hearts be far from it. Because of what God allowed me to see, I could say, "God bless you, and I release you to do God's work." I was no longer a stumbling block for them, and they were no longer a frustration to me.

Deception

Remember, the person betraying me would say things to my family to gain sympathy. A deceiver tries to gain support and empathy from those closest to you. Watch out for people who are overly helpful, trying to win the hearts of the people.

Deceivers also blend in with others. Especially once they feel you may be on to them. Once they know that you notice them, they blend in. Sometimes, people in the church say little; they just move around. Lay before the Lord in prayer, and the Holy Spirit will reveal the deceivers.

Watch out for these five "Ds":
disrespect, dishonesty, disobedience,
double vision, and deception.

Make sure you don't give a deceiver too much information.

I would give out information without realizing that it could harm me or the ministry. Deceivers run with information to help complete their agenda. They forget that God sent them to help. Some will get close to you so that they can get information on people in the church or to look for ways to advance themselves.

Now, many leaders work alone because it is hard to trust even those that are in ministry. But we must trust God and ask him to help our leaders. If you are working under a leader, do all your work unto the Lord with a clean heart and a right spirit.

Some deceivers would go through my husband to get him to share information or get what they needed through him. In these cases, my ears had to be just as keen as my eyes. Words reveal the heart. Learn to recognize the words of a deceiver.

Pray for the innocent ones.

Besides recognizing the warning signs, it's important to pray for those around the deceiver. During betrayal, you can become so focused on the deceiver that you forget to cover the innocent ones on which they prey.

The innocent ones don't know the deceiver's agenda. They are like innocent sheep who take the deceiver at their word. Pray for their eyes to be open, so deceivers will not take them away with seductive words.

For example, one of my betrayers was seemingly big on the word of God but would use it out of context to suit their agenda. They had a plan to take people from the church to start their ministry, and the only way they could do it was to use the word of God to match their agenda. They would tell church members, "Maybe we can have Bible study at my home. I can help you understand the Bible." They were aggressively nice because they had an agenda. Be sure to bring the word of God back to the people, so deceivers do not mislead them.

When deceivers come into the ministry, they find an area they can exploit, saying things like, "There's nobody over this ministry so I can take it over to establish myself." After they get the microphone or a certificate to preach, you see their true colors. It's amazing how someone can "give the word" or preach a sermon, and then, their whole disposition changes.

Watch out for people who change after they receive a title or position. Pride comes before a fall. People who have been in the ministry for years can suddenly change once you give them a microphone. Now, I don't give people keys to the building or a microphone until they can serve, clean, and humble themselves. I had to learn the hard way!

If you are a leader, protect the flock (the congregation) from people like this. Learn to recognize the warning signs and confront them, speaking the truth in love and with wisdom. The Holy Spirit will show you the deceivers in your midst, so don't let your heart be troubled.

✓ KEEP YOUR EMOTIONS IN CHECK! DON'T LET YOUR HEART BE TROUBLED.

Chapter 6: Don't Let Your Heart Be Troubled

*Let not your heart be troubled: ye believe in
God, believe also in me. (John 14:1 KJV)*

*But the Comforter, which is the Holy Ghost,
whom the Father will send in my name, he shall
teach you all things, and bring all things to your
remembrance, whatsoever I have said unto you.
²⁷ Peace I leave with you, my peace I give unto
you: not as the world giveth, give I unto you. Let
not your heart be troubled, neither let it be
afraid. (John 14:26-27 KJV)*

It is painful to accept that someone you groomed and
trained is your betrayer. You may have been
thinking about the part they would play in bringing
your vision to pass, or how they would be a help to you
in the years ahead. And then, suddenly, you discover
they have instead been delaying the vision—it's enough

to make your heart troubled and discouraged. However, when the Holy Spirit reveals the betrayal, it rescues you from giving your heart to someone who is unworthy of it.

So don't let your heart be troubled; put it in check and let go. Don't hold on to deceivers and betrayers—even when you have invested in them—let them go. Yes, you may have poured into them, but realize that they have misused your time, treasure, and anointing. It's time to let go—don't let betrayal trouble your heart.

The pain is real, but God has something greater for you and inside of you. You don't always see the greatness when you have a "knife in our back," and the pain still stings. But betrayal stirs up the greatness on the inside of you. He can use the situation to cause you to rise to the occasion and mature.

Guard your heart and sanctify it with the word of God.

Above all else, guard your heart, for everything you do flows from it. (Proverbs 4:23 NIV) Sometimes, you have to pray people and the hurt they have caused out of your heart. If not, you can operate out of bitterness in response. And that can contaminate everything you do because everything you do flows from your heart.

You have probably experienced someone who operates out of bitterness and pain, and know it's not a pleasant experience. When you're ministering out of hurt, two things can happen. You can push people into a place

God did not intend for them to go and do the same to yourself. You can drive good people away because they can't take the toxicity anymore. Also, if you don't let go of deceivers, you will try to fit people into a vision God never intended them to support. Moreover, you can damage yourself. It can damage your joy and your physical health.

When your heart is in despair, turn to the word of God and the Holy Spirit for encouragement. Keep the plans of God before you, so what he intended to happen will manifest. Betrayal doesn't change God's commitment to your purpose and destiny. That is the time to pull on God's strength. Accept the truth of the word of God—not for other people—but yourself.

Consider the life of Joseph. His brothers betrayed him; they sold him into slavery and threw him into a pit. If he had remained in the pit and forgotten the dream, he would have died. Even though you may be in a low place you don't want to be, know God is taking you to the next level. Joseph didn't have anybody around him; we have to be okay with God removing people from our lives.

His brothers were with him in the house, but they couldn't go with him to the palace. Joseph needed to be alone in the pit to get to the palace. That was God's ordained plan; he never intended for Joseph to be in the pit forever. Even in pain, accept the truth of who you are, and who God has called you to be, so you don't get stuck in the pit.

The pain and agony are not intended to last forever.

When people leave, believe something better is coming. Trust God. The people with you today may not be with you five years from now. Look at the bigger picture, learn from it, and become wise.

Joseph had to learn how to govern and be a great leader. The betrayal and the pit were part of the process, part of the bigger picture. He began as a dreamer with a vision from God and a coat of many colors from his biological father. Remember the vision while you're in the pit. Understand that there is something greater, and the pit is a pit stop to destiny.

The pit is a pit stop to destiny.

Joseph remembered the dream. You can't focus on the pit. If you want to go through the process, focus on the dream—the vision. And remember, the pit doesn't change the fact that you have the favor. The coat of many colors still belongs to you, and you are who the Heavenly Father says you are.

You are what the word of God says you are.

Even when people were trying to advance their agendas, the favor of God was still evident in Joseph's life. He entered Potiphar's house as a slave but became the head of the house. He entered the prison as an inmate but became its manager. People can see the anointing and the favor on you, and they pull on you because of what you have.

Joseph's brothers knew that his dream was real, and it was getting on their nerves. Joseph thought he was safe with his inner circle (safe among his brothers), but because of the anointing on his life, his brothers wanted to take him out. You are not experiencing betrayal because you did something wrong. Favor and anointing can bring betrayal. So know that you are what the word of God says you are.

The vision does not change because people leave or betray you.

> Then the Lord answered me and said: "Write the vision And make it plain on tablets, That he may run who reads it. [3] For the vision is yet for an appointed time; But at the end it will speak, and it will not lie. Though it tarries, wait for it; Because it will surely come, It will not tarry. (Habakkuk 2:2-3 NKJV)

Don't build your life or vision on people, because if they betray you, then your whole vision is gone. When people leave you, keep it moving! It's not the vision that leaves; it's a person. Vision doesn't have a face. Don't lose sight of the vision. You are still the visionary, and the vision is still God-given. There's life after betrayal. There's life after that person leaves you.

My biological father left us, didn't return my letters, or tell me he wanted to see me until I was eighteen because he didn't want to pay child support. I could have used all of that to justify not succeeding. Now I realize your destiny is not tied to your past but the future. My father was part of my past. I didn't have to bring his negative impact into my future.

Take that truth and run with it. If God has to call people from another state or country, he will bring people to support the vision. He will get people to you that are supposed to be a part of your vision. He's not a man that he should lie; anything he said will happen.

People who are supposed to be part of your vision are the ones who can run with it. Some people may preach down the house, but if they can't run with the vision, they may cause more damage than good. Some people had been with me several years who were not motivated, but new people came in ready to get things done.

If you can't get someone even to pick up a piece of paper, keep moving and know that they are not part of the vision. If it's not in people to support the vision, you can't make them. Perhaps they are still carrying the vision of the house they came from and have not fully embraced yours. People who are supposed to be a part of the vision come motivated.

Keep the bigger picture, the broader vision before you. Instead of asking, "Why me?" don't let your heart be troubled and focus on the vision. There is greater coming.

✓ **KEEP YOUR EMOTIONS IN CHECK. STOP ASKING WHY.**

CHAPTER 7: STOP ASKING WHY

"Lord, why is this happening to me? I mean, maybe they didn't know what they were doing?"

When something negative happened, I immediately tried to figure out why. I would question the person's motive, asking, "Why are they doing that? Why don't they understand? Do they know what they are doing? Are they doing it intentionally? Why is this happening?"

It's natural to have questions when things go wrong. But anybody who wants to be like Jesus is a perfect candidate for betrayal. Although the pain is heavy, you are the perfect candidate. When you embrace that reality, you can say, "Not my will Lord, but yours be done." Take responsibility for going through your process so God can get the glory, and others may see him high and lifted.

The attack comes to you individually, but how you respond affects other people. The enemy's greater agenda is to stop what God wants to do in your family, ministry, or future. If you can't forgive, it will affect your family. If you allow a deceiver to lead or operate within your ministry, it may affect innocent members. God trusts you to respond appropriately to betrayal, protect those around you, and accomplish his will.

With that in mind, the question becomes, "Why not me?" Jesus was the perfect candidate because he had neither spot nor blemish. He was the perfect, sacrificial lamb slain before the foundation of the world. Jesus was at all points tempted as we are, yet he did not sin. He didn't deserve betrayal, but he was its perfect candidate. He endured it for the sake of others—for our sake.

When you are tempted to ask, "Lord, why me?" read Jesus' words and see how Jesus handled betrayal. His life will give you the wisdom to know when to speak and confront, and when to be quiet. Walk very closely with God during these times. He is your invisible support as you walk the tightrope called betrayal. You can't do it without his presence. You will come out stronger and better if you walk closely with him.

Jesus was betrayed and crucified for us. Are you willing to be crucified with Christ? If we suffer, we shall also reign with him: if we deny him, he also will deny us. (2 Timothy 2:12 KJV)

I no longer call you slaves, because a master doesn't confide in his slaves. Now you are my friends since I have told you everything the Father told me. (John 15:15 NLT)

It's easy to be someone's friend when there's no trouble, calamity, or crisis. Christians sing the song, "I am a friend of God." We cry out, "God use me!" But when Jesus is looking for someone to use during these times, to stick it out with him in the furnace of affliction, he often finds people that have forgotten that they are the perfect candidate.

Jesus was the first candidate. His life testifies that you can have victory over betrayal and come out better on the other side of the process. He rose on the third day with triumph and victory. It's an honor for God to use you; it's an honor to emulate Christ.

Longsuffering is a fruit of the Spirit, and betrayal can grow that fruit in your life and character. Nobody picks the fruit of longsuffering from the tree. Don't leave longsuffering on the branch forever. Jesus showed us how to eat that fruit. You see his demonstration of longsuffering in the word of God.

Longsuffering is a fruit of the Spirit, and betrayal can grow that fruit in your life and character.

If you have been chosen to go through betrayal, you have been selected to be more like him. It means he trusted you enough to go through betrayal. He chose you as a candidate—that's an honor. So thank him for the opportunity. Instead of asking God why, ask the Holy

Spirit how to move on. He will give you the wisdom to minimize the damage to all parties affected and safeguard what you've already built in the ministry. Ask him for wisdom to handle people and their behaviors.

Some people need deliverance; others need development.

Sometimes people do wrong, but their motive is innocent. I've had to work with many people with no ministry experience. They may do wrong, but it's an innocent mistake. While others who say they have ministry experience intentionally do harm. From experience, I have concluded that some people need deliverance; others need development.

Remember, Judas walked with Jesus for years. You can't always throw people away the moment they betray you. Sometimes, they may have an innocent heart and lack the knowledge and skill to do what is right—they need development. Other times, they need deliverance. Either way, if they are not willing to change their character, then that is when I disallow them from operating in ministry. I can't allow the wrong spirit to contaminate what I've already built. Even if I need what they offer, I won't move on it until it's coming from a clean place—a right spirit. What they offer may look good on the outside, but it will tear down the house later. The Holy Spirit will give you wisdom. Ask. He will provide the strategy you need to use based on the individual.

There are times you will have to discipline people in ministry. Protect the vision, the work that's already been invested, and the people of the house. The Holy Spirit will give you strategies. Go beyond asking why and ask for wisdom for the journey.

You must prepare for the journey.

Once you know that you are being betrayed, prepare yourself. Each morning you prepare to leave home; you know certain things must be in place. You would not leave the house without taking a shower and having your driver's license, etc. If it's winter season, you know you need a coat, or a hat and gloves. Similarly, if you know you're in a season of betrayal, make sure you have certain things in place such as a strong prayer life, an obedient heart to do the Father's will, and the word of God operating in your life.

This season requires the word of God. You will need time for the word of God and the Holy Spirit to sanctify you before you stand before people to minister or serve.

You've got to understand that on this journey, there is no turning back. You've got to be mentally and spiritually prepared. And you need every spiritual gift there is as well as the fruit of the Spirit. You need love, joy, peace, and patience daily for this journey.

Don't leave the house without acknowledging the Holy Spirit, asking for his leading, guidance, direction, and correction. Don't think you won't make any errors or have wrong thinking about a person or thing. You will need the Holy Spirit's correction because you will want to strike back and tell everybody about your betrayer.

But you have to allow God to walk you through this and work with you on this one.

Betrayal is a spiritual battle, and losing is not an option. You have to come out a winner. It reminds me of when he sent the disciples out, and he said, take nothing of your own with you (purse or script). When you go on this journey, you can't take anything of your own; the flesh cannot walk with you on this journey. You wrestle not against flesh and blood.

And you're not alone. Jesus sent them out two by two. So it's you and the Holy Spirit. He will bring people along your path to let you know he's with you, and you're not alone.

When you go on a journey, you have to make sure your vehicle is gassed up. You can't finish this journey without being filled with the Holy Spirit. Make sure you're gassed up for the ride. If you get empty along the way, stop—and fill yourself up again with the word of God.

The anointing you had yesterday may not be enough to get you to where you need to be a month from now. So let God pour his Spirit on you continually, meditate on the word of God, and let him fill you back up in his presence (in prayer and study). Keep it moving!

✓ **KEEP YOUR EMOTIONS IN CHECK. KEEP IT MOVING AND RIDE THE DONKEY.**

Chapter 8: Ride the Donkey

Look! Your king is coming, riding on a donkey's colt!

> *The next day a great multitude that had come to the feast, when they heard that Jesus was coming to Jerusalem, [13] took branches of palm trees and went out to meet Him, and cried out: "Hosanna! 'Blessed is He who comes in the name of the Lord!' The King of Israel!" [14] Then Jesus, when He had found a young donkey, sat on it; as it is written: [15] "Fear not, daughter of Zion; Behold, your King is coming, sitting on a donkey's colt."* (John 12:12-15 NKJV)

Once you have prepared for the journey and started on your way, don't deviate from your path. Wherever and however God leads you, stay on track. The donkey is evidence that he will probably take you the way of humility. Stay the course.

The donkey symbolizes the way to your destiny, the path

that will bring God glory. It's also the vehicle to get you from where you are, to your destination—the center of God's will. You may have wanted a Porsche, something more attractive and pleasing to the eyes of man, but Jesus rode on a donkey. Are you willing to follow his lead?

The donkey is a very loyal animal. With Balaam (Numbers 22), the donkey tried to get him to stay on the right path, to remain in the place that God would have him. But when the donkey laid down, he got out and beat the donkey.

> So Balaam rose in the morning, saddled his donkey, and went with the princes of Moab. [22] Then God's anger was aroused because he went, and the Angel of the Lord took His stand in the way as an adversary against him. And he was riding on his donkey, and his two servants were with him. [23] Now the donkey saw the Angel of the Lord standing in the way with His drawn sword in His hand, and the donkey turned aside out of the way and went into the field. So Balaam struck the donkey to turn her back onto the road. [24] Then the Angel of the Lord stood in a narrow path between the vineyards, with a wall on this side and a wall on that side. [25] And when the donkey saw the Angel of the Lord, she pushed herself against the wall and crushed Balaam's foot against the wall; so he struck her again. [26] Then the Angel of the Lord went further and stood in a narrow place where there was no way to turn either to the right hand or to the left. [27] And when the donkey saw the Angel of the

Lord, she lay down under Balaam; so Balaam's anger was aroused, and he struck the donkey with his staff. ²⁸ Then the Lord opened the mouth of the donkey, and she said to Balaam, "What have I done to you, that you have struck me these three times?" ²⁹ And Balaam said to the donkey, "Because you have abused me. I wish there were a sword in my hand, for now I would kill you!" ³⁰ So the donkey said to Balaam, "Am I not your donkey on which you have ridden, ever since I became yours, to this day? Was I ever disposed to do this to you?" And he said, "No." (Numbers 22:21-30 NKJV)

Sometimes, you want to get off the donkey for the wrong reasons—you don't think it's the right vehicle, the right journey, or where you need to be. You'd rather be riding a Tesla, but the humble donkey will carry you and be faithful. God will take you through the low times. Like Balaam, if God doesn't want you to do something, he has a way of telling the donkey not to move in the direction you want to go. But if that donkey is still moving, then you ride that donkey—stay on the path God has chosen.

Before Jesus rode into Jerusalem, he told his disciples to tell the owner of the donkey to loose it because he needed it. Jesus understood that he was about to take a journey to the cross. He could have jumped off the donkey when he thought about the death that awaited him. However, he knew this was the path to bring God glory. Jesus was taking ownership of what God was about to do. It was well with him that a donkey was God's choice for him to fulfill prophesy. He was fulfilling his destiny so that God could get greater glory.

In every area of our lives, we have to learn to be okay with God's choices and ride them out. Don't be so quick to jump off, give up, give in, or ever complain about the tools God is using to get you to your purpose. The vehicle doesn't matter, as long we stay for the ride and get to our purpose at the right time—destiny and timing work together. We can delay our purpose if we get off the donkey, beat it, and chastise it because we think there should be another tool to get where we are going.

Many people had heard Jesus declare himself king, the son of God. They thought he came to establish an earthly kingdom, so they didn't expect him to enter Jerusalem riding on a humble donkey. Jesus knew whose hosanna was genuine and whose were not.

Watch those around you.

When you're on the donkey, people are watching. When you're going down a path, many are looking for you to die or get off course. Sometimes, we're shameful of our situations. We don't like people to see us ridiculed, oppressed, laughed at, and mocked. It can be humiliating and humbling, especially when those who used to cheer you on are now whispering about you on the sidelines.

They say one thing to your face, but in their heart, it's something different. In your time of testing, people change. The same disciples who said they would never leave Jesus ran off during his time to fulfill his purpose.

Be observant when you're riding the donkey. You will gain insight into the nature of people. Watch the expressions of the people around you.

All eyes are on you when you're riding the donkey.

If you watch, you will notice that some people waited for this moment for you. They were waiting for you to be in a humiliating predicament. When they're looking at it one way, you should be looking at it differently. Your attitude should be, "I'm about to save all of you. I'm about to do something that many don't think I'm capable of doing. And God is about to show you all his glory—even though I'm the one on the donkey. You are looking at me one way, but it's for your good that I remain on this donkey."

When Jesus was on that donkey, he knew his suffering was for the betterment—the salvation—of the people watching him from the sidelines. I would pray for the people around me amid betrayal because I did not want it to affect them negatively. When you know that a person is deceiving you, and out to kill you, your character, and ministry, you want to get off the donkey; you want to call them out on their wickedness and let them know that you see what they're doing. But I had to learn to stay and remain on the donkey in my life and my marriage.

When my husband and I separated, I had asked him to leave the house. But I realized that to bring God glory and allow my son to see what a real marriage looked like, I had to swallow a pill that I never expected. I never, ever thought I could swallow it because it wasn't a part of my character. I had to swallow the pill called pride.

I was ready to get a divorce, but God did not allow me. My husband was already out of the house, and the Holy Spirit dealt with me one night. The Holy Spirit said, "You're not doing it my way. You'll never get to where I'm taking you."

I didn't see my husband coming home as part of my process. I thought, "This thing can damage a person or cause them to lose their mind, but you're saying stay on the donkey?" I said, "I can't do this one." Everybody was saying my husband was great, but I was like, "This is Judas (so I thought), don't you know he's betraying me!" To them, something was wrong with me because they saw a different picture. I saw my husband behind closed doors. However, something happened with my son, and that brought us back together. To see what God has done in my marriage is truly amazing. There were so many odds against our marriage.

Don't get off your donkey.

If I had gotten off the donkey, I would have messed up many people, and I'm not even sure if I would have been happy. Yes, it would have been an easy way out for me; it would have been less stressful to get off the donkey. But I had to trust God beyond what I could see—literally trust him as if I were in a life and death situation.

I couldn't see him loving me so much and allowing me to go through so much pain. I couldn't imagine him not knowing what was going on in the ministry.

Eventually, I refused to stress out because of betrayal, people, and things because he knows that there is greater. There's something he has that's greater. My sons needed to see a successful marriage, and God has turned my marriage around. That was bigger than my emotions or betrayal.

Stay on your path. Ride your donkey so that God can get the glory!

✓ **KEEP YOUR EMOTIONS IN CHECK. YOU CAN BE USED, BUT NOT COME OUT BRUISED.**

CHAPTER 9: BE USED NOT BRUISED

After the donkey, there was the cross.

And about the ninth hour Jesus cried with a loud voice, saying, Eli, Eli, lama sabachthani? that is to say, My God, my God, why hast thou forsaken me? (Matthew 27:46 KJV)

Jesus rode the donkey. He endured the bumpy ride, but after that was the cross. Jesus had some apprehension about bearing the cross, asking if the cup could pass from him. In the end, he declared, "Nevertheless, not my will, but yours be done." Knowing a painful experience awaits the end of your ride can cause fear.

Fear will keep you from going forward. But you can be afraid and still go through the process to overcome the fear. Sometimes, you have to take the first step while you're still scared. Just don't come down from your cross experience.

On the cross, you're naked before people. Everybody is looking up to you, and you're exposed. Your emotions and everything inside of you is in disarray. You're vulnerable; you are hurt.

I'm sure all those lashes Jesus took, and the nails in his hands had to hurt. That's why he was bleeding. Even Jesus bled. So when people go through betrayal, it hurts. Our hearts bleed; it's painful.

Often, we don't want to go through it—not all the way. Jesus went to the very end—all the way—through the donkey ride to the cross. Some of us want to get on the donkey but not journey to the cross.

---

*Some of us want to get on the donkey
but not journey to the cross.*

Jesus had to see the disciples walk out on him. He saw Peter deny him, and the disciples run away. Some people closest to you will deny they ever knew you when things happen in your life. They will leave you. He sat there, and he hung on the cross. He saw all of it; his eyes were not closed to it. He saw all the betrayal.

You can't close your eyes either when you are on this journey, or when you are vulnerable and naked. We overcome by our testimony (and the blood of the lamb). So even in the processes we go through, we can't be ashamed of the pathways we had to take for God's glory. We cannot be embarrassed because it's a good thing to be used. Again, I count it as an honor and a privilege for him to use me.

But to go all the way to the cross means enduring abandonment, rejection, and shame. But the beauty of it is coming out used but not bruised. They crucified Jesus, but they did not break any of his bones. Yes, you were used, and you bled, but you shouldn't walk away with broken bones. When God heals you, everything can still be in tack—still whole. Nothing broken. Nothing missing.

Don't allow shame to break you.

When you're on the cross, just being there for everyone to see your nakedness is fearful and shameful. Often, we feel shame about what we're going through (about being betrayed), but there's no one to blame because God allowed it. Shame can make you angry. You want to focus on the betrayer and what's wrong with them. But all the betrayals can work together for your good.

When I looked at everything that had happened—from my dad to my husband to people in the church—it was so shameful. I don't think people realized how ashamed I was. I looked good on the outside, but I carried a lot of guilt for what I had gone through and was still going through. Not being loved as a child by my father was shameful. My mother and I were close. She had such a big heart to raise seven children; she knew what every child needed. Still, she goes out of her way for every child, remembering every child's and grandchild's birthday. She went out of her way to love.

But there was something about me that wanted my father's love. I did not get it, and I felt ashamed not to have a father. Mentally, I knew my father existed, but I was ashamed not to have received his love. I couldn't even say I spent a summer with him or even knew his side of the family. To this day, I don't know any of his people. My mom and her mother are the only people I got to know. So I felt like a part of me was missing, and I was ashamed because of that.

I was ashamed of my relationship with my husband. There was no togetherness; there was nothing of substance. There was only arguing and turmoil. I was different at home than outside. Everybody knew me one way on the outside. I would get home, and it would be so different. I had a struggle with who I was and the path I was taking.

God was using me in ministry, but I wasn't fit for use because rejection and abandonment broke me. I could preach (give what the Holy Spirit had given me), and people would be so excited. But I couldn't remember what I said after I sat down. I would come back home broken and angry because I didn't feel like I could be proud of my life. When I came home, I had to fight within myself to stay alive for the next day.

God used betrayal to take me to my own personal cross. It was a place where I surrendered; I allowed God to use me so that others would live. When you come through an experience like that—when you're resurrected—the pain doesn't sting like it did when you were going through the process. It's like a woman in labor. The pain is real, just like the birthing pains of ministry. But once the baby comes, there's joy. When you realize that God has used your betrayal for his glory, you don't have to stay bruised; you can be better.

The beauty of betrayal is when you can come out of betrayal, stronger, wiser, and more than you thought you could ever be. Hopefully, as we have journeyed together through this book, and along your path, there has been some deliverance. I had to come to grips with my emotions and die to myself to not be bitter and mad at my betrayers. Ironically, I now have so much love for them.

When you realize that God has used your betrayal for his glory, you don't have to stay bruised; you can be better. The beauty of betrayal is when you can come out of betrayal, stronger, wiser, and more than you thought you could ever be.

The beauty of betrayal is also coming out used but not bruised. I would never have known what was on the inside of me. I would not have known the strength that I had on the inside to go through it, nor the spirits that could not stay with me—they had to go, or I could not fulfill God's purpose. So much had to die and come out of me so it would not permanently bruise me.

Now, it's a new morning. Because of betrayal, I have revelation and experience with God that freed me from my past. Letting go of the past and letting God work freed me in many areas of my life. Before, I wanted to blame everybody that had hurt me. But I couldn't because this is the path he allowed to happen in my life. Once I finally came to grips with that, it was okay with my soul. When I healed, it helped my husband to heal.

I was freer. I wasn't ashamed to be me anymore. The guilt and shame lifted off of me. Thank you, Lord! The path he used for me to get to the place where I could see a new morning is amazing!

After the darkness, every night always bring a new morning.

Once you have gone through that darkness, conquered fear, and hung on the cross, it's a new morning. When you're in Christ, you will not die; a new day is dawning. That morning after the Resurrection, they thought Jesus was dead; but there are new mercies every morning.

Morning is the break of a new revelation. You don't have to wait for the next day. You can have a morning experience right now. Revelation gives you enlightenment, it brings light to your situation, and a new light has come your way.

Embrace the revelation of the new you who has come through betrayal. You can conquer fear! Know that your beginning is just starting. People thought it would take you out or kill you, but you are just beginning to live.

Receive a new revelation of who you are. It's time to move past your past.

> ✓ KEEP YOUR EMOTIONS IN CHECK. MOVE PAST THE PAST.

CHAPTER 10: MOVE PAST THE PAST

> *And after eight days again his disciples were within, and Thomas with them: then came Jesus, the doors being shut, and stood in the midst, and said, Peace be unto you. [27] Then saith he to Thomas, Reach hither thy finger, and behold my hands; and reach hither thy hand, and thrust it into my side: and be not faithless, but believing. (John 20:26-27 KJV)*

Jesus could show Thomas the holes from his nail-pierced hands. Evidence of his scars was still in his physical body, but he was spiritually and mentally healed. He didn't come back talking about the pain of what had happened to him but the power of what he had overcome—resurrection power.

You should also come out of betrayal with supernatural empowerment to conquer greater things. Let go of the past and look to the future, your destiny, God's plan, and purpose.

If betrayal couldn't take you out, then nothing can stop you. You can now conquer any and everything. You have the reassurance of the Holy Spirit, his power, and might. Jesus said he could have called on angels, but he went through the process because he knew there were greater things he was leaving for us.

He left us resurrection power.

You had to go through betrayal not only for yourself but so that other people may also see the glory of God. Now, you have the power to reproduce disciples, to get people to a place of power. After you come through betrayal and deceit, it should change you. There's no way God can take you through a process, and not change you.

After going through the pain and process, you can talk as an overcomer. You can speak from the standpoint of a victor—not a victim. The beauty of betrayal is transformation. It changes you forever. You're walking in newness, power, revelation, and wisdom.

After you confront deep issues of rejection, shame, and abandonment, there's an entirely new person who emerges that you have to learn. Learn this new person because the transformation is so powerful.

You don't even think, walk, and talk the same. Your ears don't hear the same, and eyes don't see the same. That's the resurrection power that comes when God has used you for his glory. He changes your identity altogether. Get to know the new you.

With this resurrection power, you have every spiritual weapon that you need. And now you know how to use spiritual weapons without retaliation or revenge. You're careful how you use them because you don't want to abuse the power that God has given you. Jesus had power before he went to the cross, but he got up with resurrection power. So now, when you go through things, and people try to deceive you again, it's not like the first time they betrayed you. Because you're careful, and you have more wisdom and knowledge to deal with it than before. You don't even tolerate the same things the same way.

When you've gone through, and you overcome, the hurt fades. It takes away the sting. I'm around people who talk about their past all the time; they can't move forward. They have a great anointing on their life, but they can't move forward—can't get past the past. When you have an encounter with God, and you're humbled and surrender to him, you come out differently!

That's transformation power! It's the power to change in form, nature, or character. When you're transformed and made over, people around you should be able to see a change in you. They should hear a difference and be able to tell that you are in a different place. It should be evident that God has moved you beyond where they knew you to be.

After the resurrection, Jesus walked through the streets, and people saw him. People should be able to see a change after you've gone through the fire, and you've gone through your cross experience.

Even your accusers, those that tried to take you out, should be able to see the new you. When that happens, it will amaze them because they will know what they have said and done. But you won't be entertaining any of those negative thoughts. You will talk about resurrection power and what God is doing in your life.

There is empowerment in leaving the past behind.

After the new morning, realize that it is finished. You have overcome the shame and agony. Because it's a new day, move past the past. It is finished.

Don't re-live it. Don't allow it to keep running in your mind. Don't fester the wound anymore. It's time to heal because pain should not last forever! Embrace the new, healed you. Move past your past.

✓ KEEP YOUR EMOTIONS IN CHECK. MOVE PAST THE PAST.

Glossary

Unforgiveness (noun)

- Merriam Webster's Dictionary lists the definition of unforgiveness as the word, unforgivingness.[1] Some argue that there is no such word as unforgiveness. It is an evolved, common usage of the original word unforgivingness, which is the noun form of unforgiving.

Unforgiving[2] (adjective)

- Unwilling or unable to forgive
- Having or making no allowance for error or weakness

---

[1] Merriam Webster's Dictionary Online, s.v. "Unforgiveness," https://www.merriam-webster.com/dictionary/unforgiveness (accessed November 6, 2019).

[2] Merriam Webster's Dictionary Online, s.v. "Unforgiving," https://www.merriam-webster.com/dictionary/unforgiving (accessed November 6, 2019).

ABOUT THE AUTHOR

Dr. Sandra B. Cook is an author, investor, entrepreneur, mentor, and founder of the Church of Restoration and Transformation. She is the daughter of Easterlin Pearl Taylor of Eastover, South Carolina, and the late Tommy Benjamin Sr. of Wilmington, Delaware. She has been married for twenty-seven years to Louis Cook, Jr. and has two sons of valor, Justin Lewis and Louis Cook, III. She retired from the Social Security Administration in 2019 to become an author and a full-time apostle.

She was an honor graduate of Benedict College, where she earned a Bachelor of Science in Accounting and continued her education to receive a Master's in Theology and a Doctorate in Ministry from Destiny Christian University, Winter Haven, Florida.

She truly understands the laboring that goes into ministering to God's people, and she has lain down her life for it. For it is written, the harvest is plentiful, but the laborers are few. Where much is given, yes, too, much is required. She has been in ministry for over twenty-eight years, and she is the founder and Apostle of The Church of Restoration and Transformation, better known as CORAT. She believes in *One God, One Faith, and One Baptism*, where restoration, transformation, and the manifestation of the power of God heals and delivers through the Holy Spirit. Nothing broken, nothing missing!

Through her humbling scripture, she declares, "I understand that God is the vine, and I am the branch: I will forever abide in him and him in me. Through him, I can bring forth much fruit: but without him, I am nothing!" (Inspired by John 15:5 KJV)

For more information about the author, visit https://www.facebook.com/Dr-Sandra-B-Cook-101388414629586/.